EASY PIANO SOLOS

BALLADS

ISBN 978-1-61774-206-4

EXCLUSIVELY DISTRIBUTED BY

Visit Hal Leonard Online at
www.halleonard.com

BEAUTIFUL

Words and Music by
LINDA PERRY

Moderately ♩ = 76

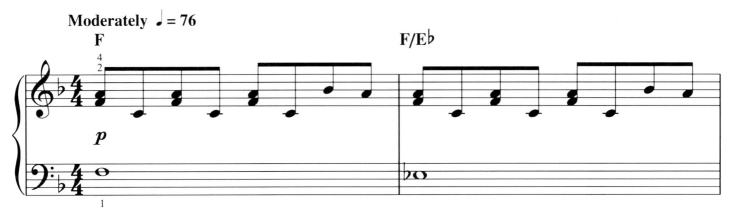

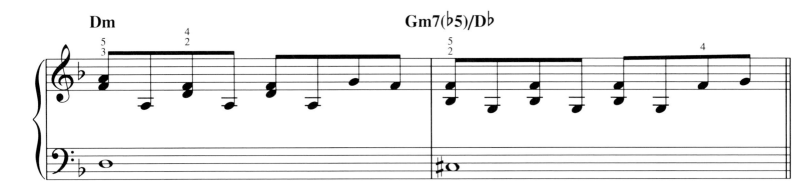

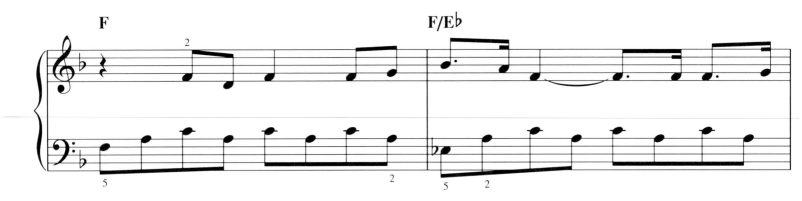

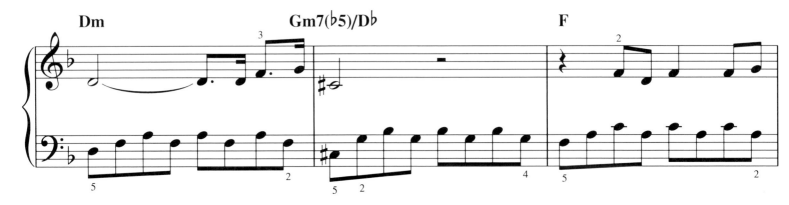

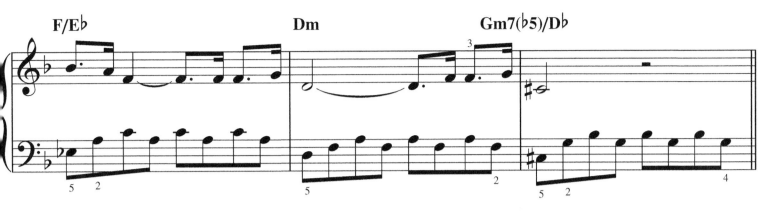

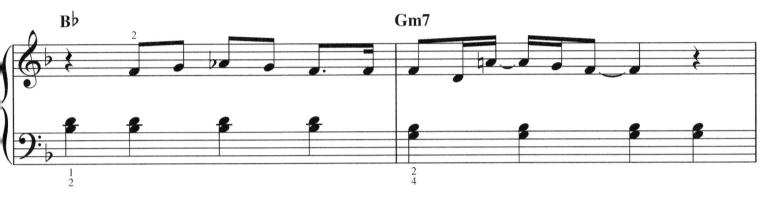

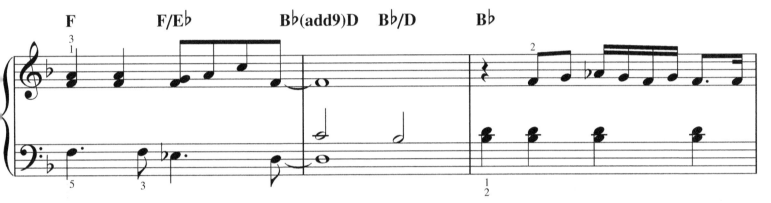

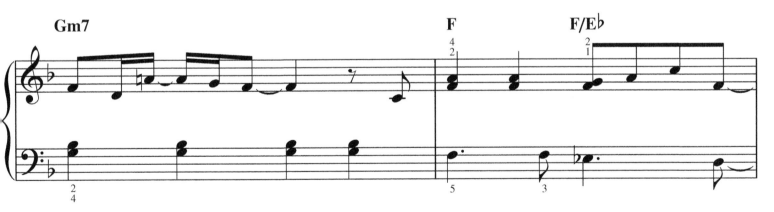

BRIDGE OVER TROUBLED WATER

Words and Music by
PAUL SIMON

In a singing style ♩ = 92

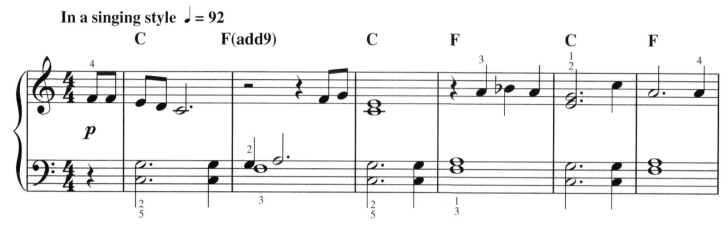

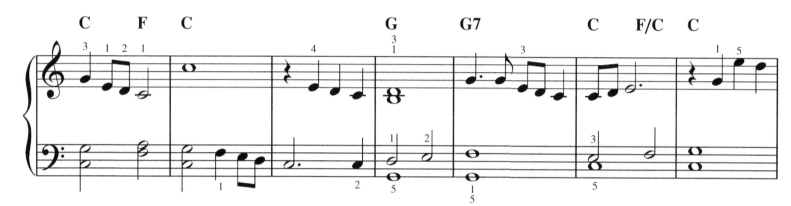

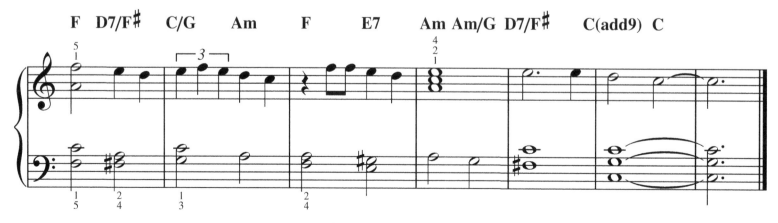

CAN'T HELP FALLING IN LOVE

from the Paramount Picture BLUE HAWAII

Words and Music by GEORGE DAVID WEISS,
HUGO PERETTI and LUIGI CREATORE

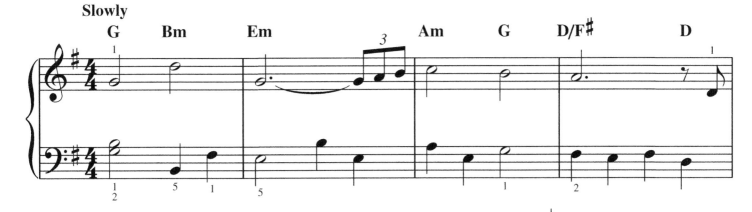

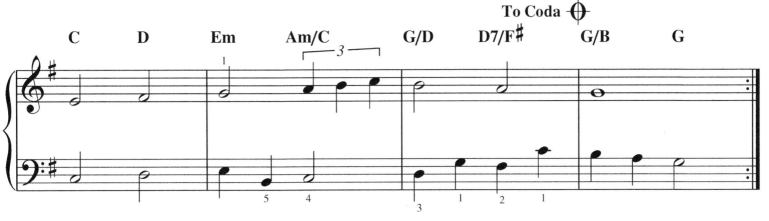

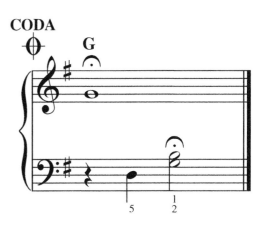

CAN'T TAKE MY EYES OFF OF YOU

Words and Music by BOB CREWE
and BOB GAUDIO

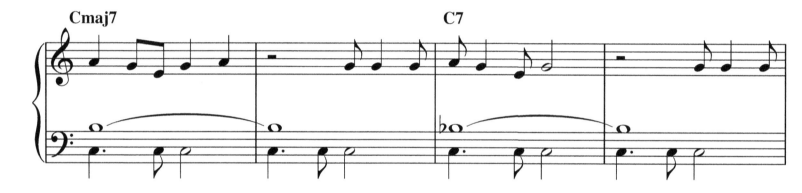

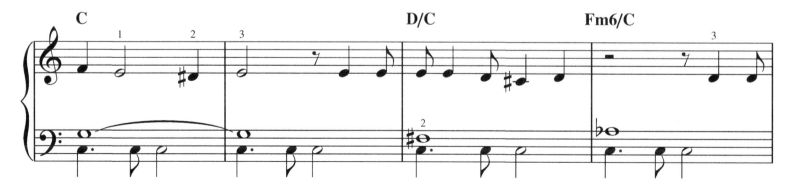

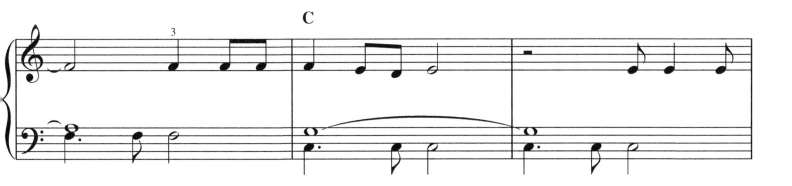

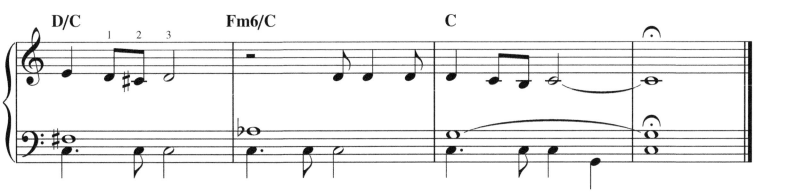

CANDLE IN THE WIND

Words and Music by ELTON JOHN
and BERNIE TAUPIN

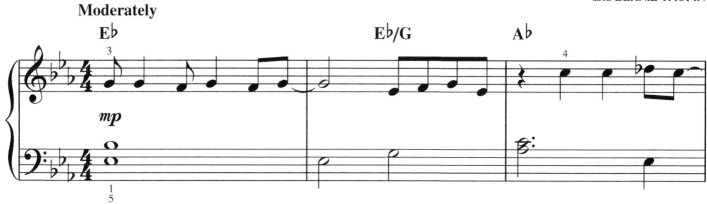

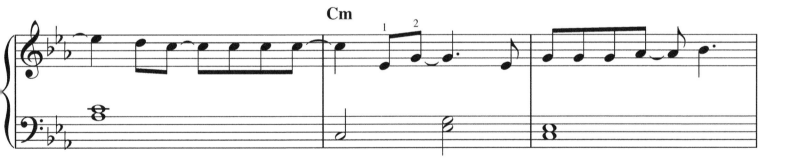

CRAZY

Words and Music by
WILLIE NELSON

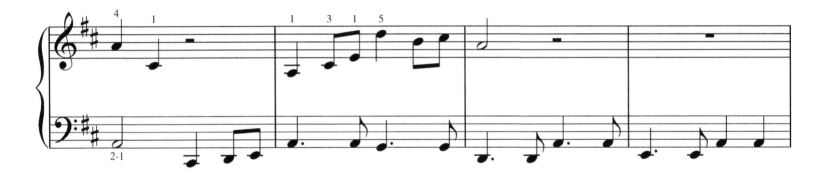

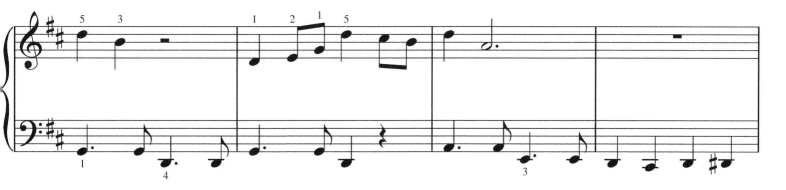

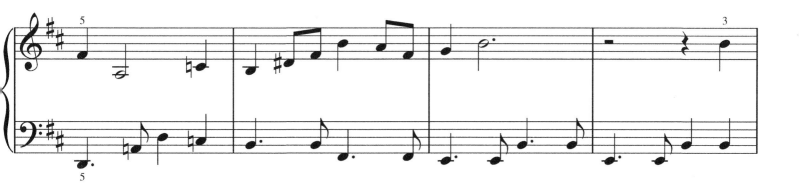

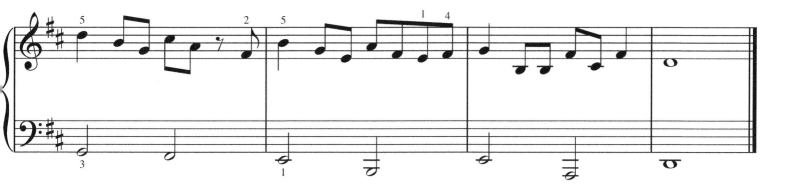

ETERNAL FLAME

Words and Music by BILLY STEINBERG,
TOM KELLY and SUSANNA HOFFS

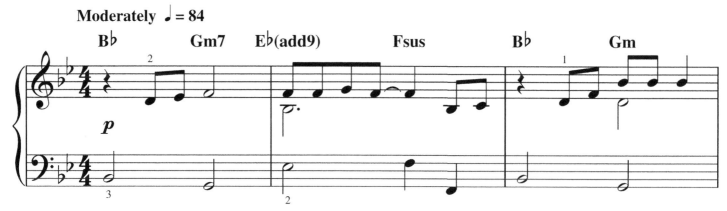

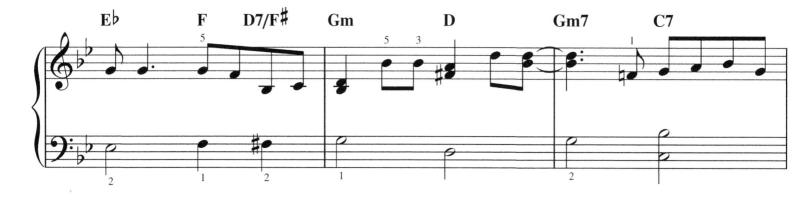

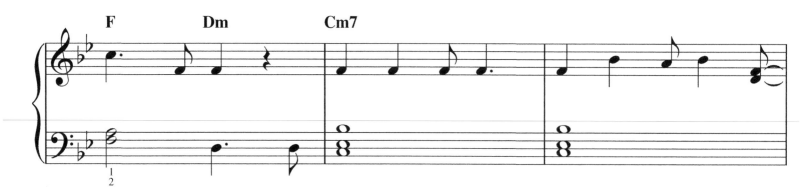

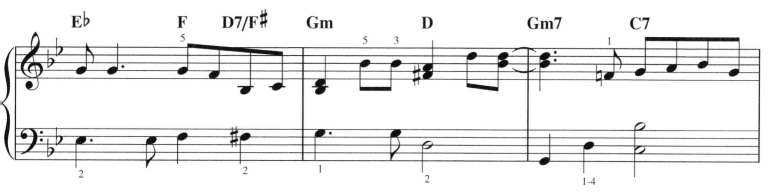

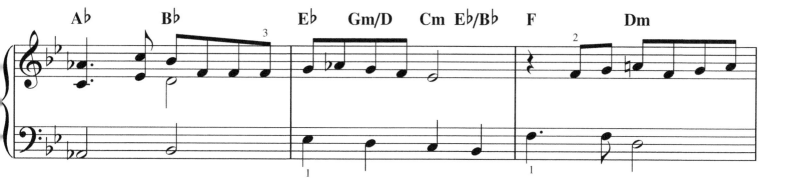

FIELDS OF GOLD

Music and Lyrics by
STING

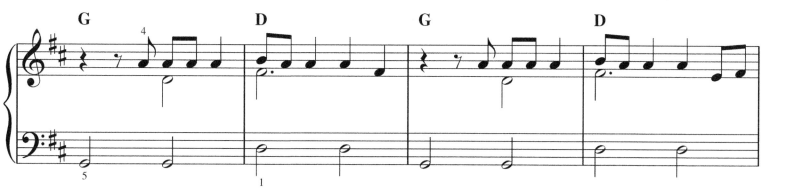

GEORGIA ON MY MIND

Words by STUART GORRELL
Music by HOAGY CARMICHAEL

Moderately, with a blues feel

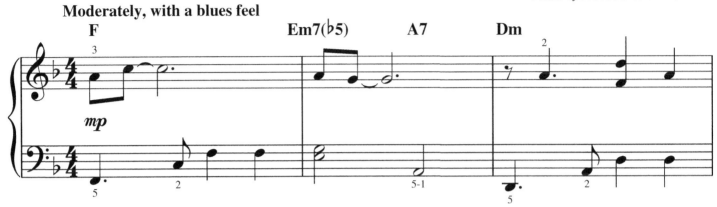

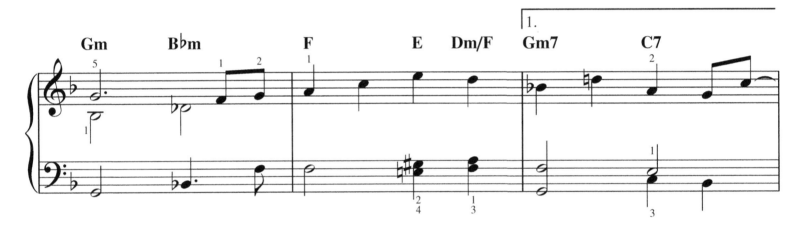

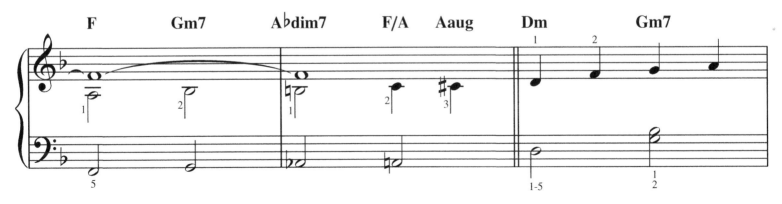

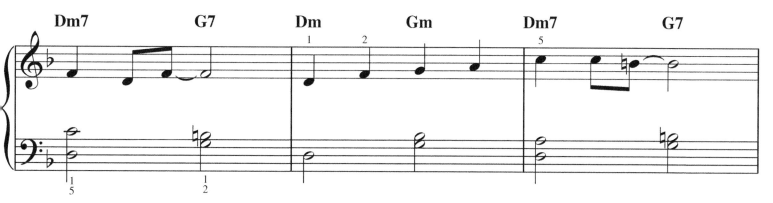

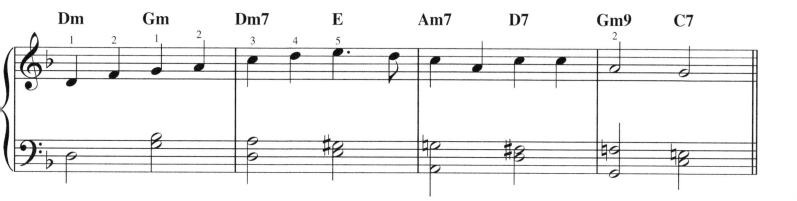

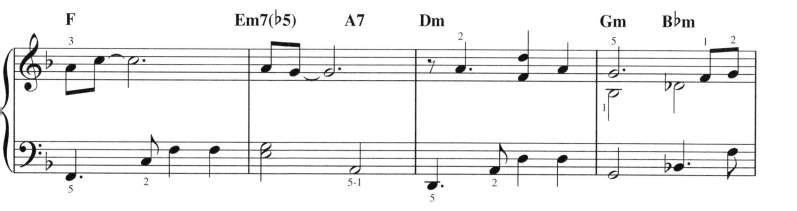

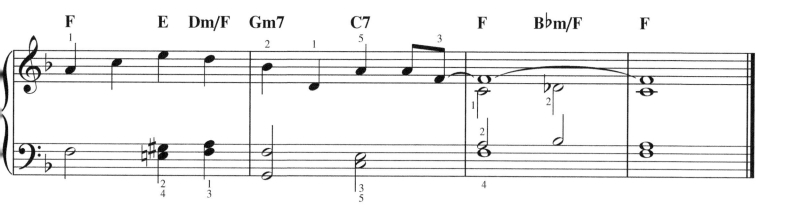

HERO

Words and Music by MARIAH CAREY
and WALTER AFANASIEFF

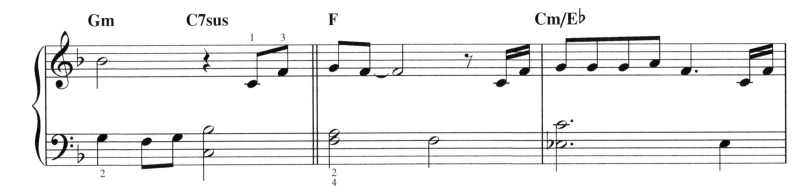

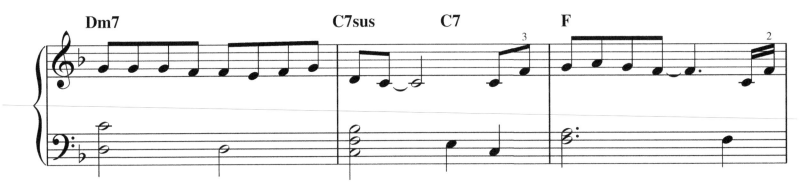

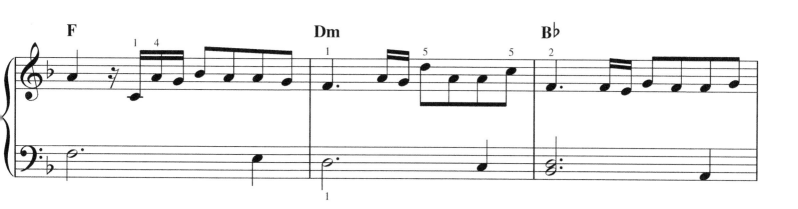

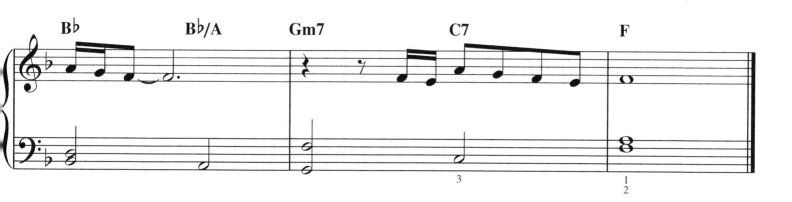

I SAY A LITTLE PRAYER

Lyric by HAL DAVID
Music by BURT BACHARACH

1st time only: D.C.
(Take 1st ending)

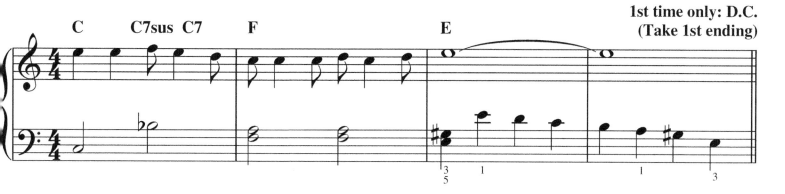

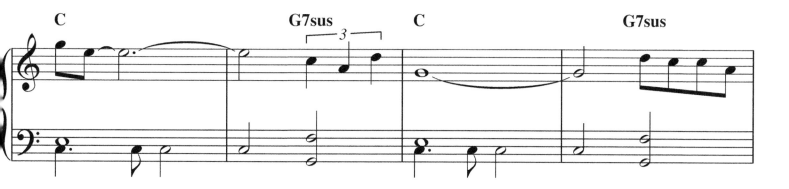

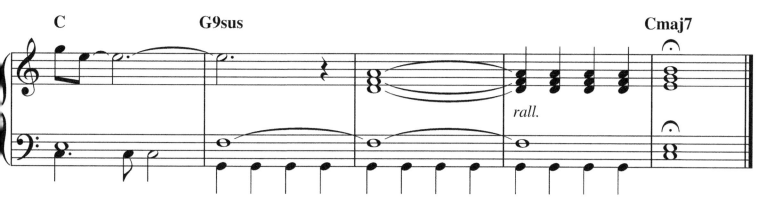

IMAGINE

Words and Music by
JOHN LENNON

Slowly

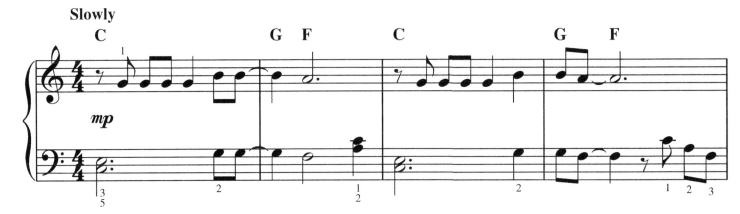

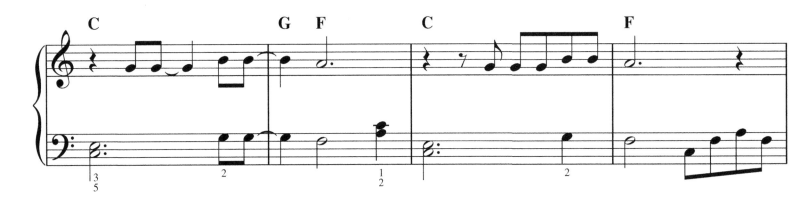

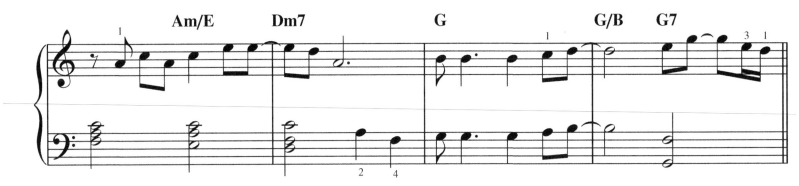

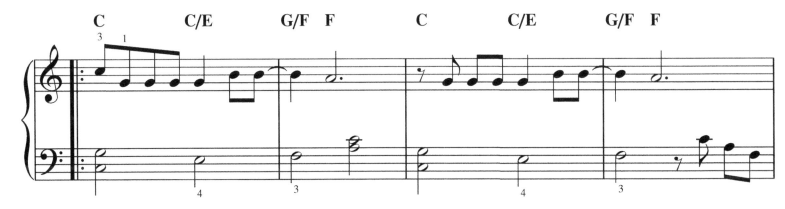

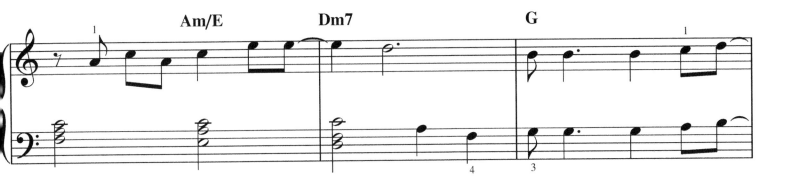

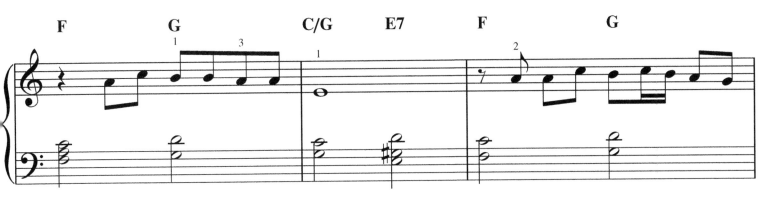

MISTY

Music by ERROLL GARNER

Slowly, with expression

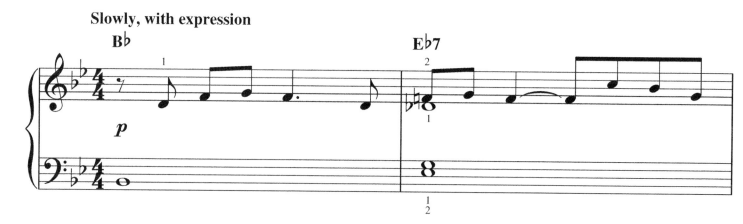

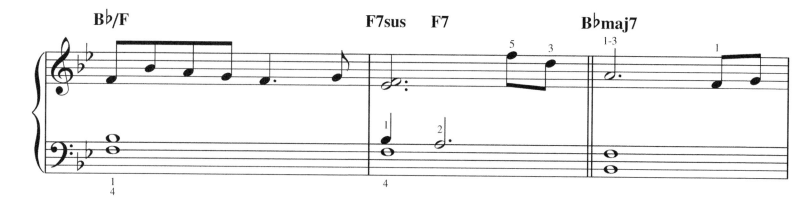

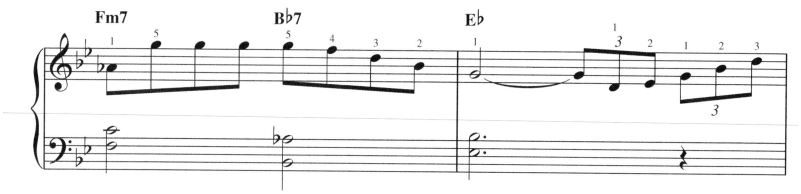

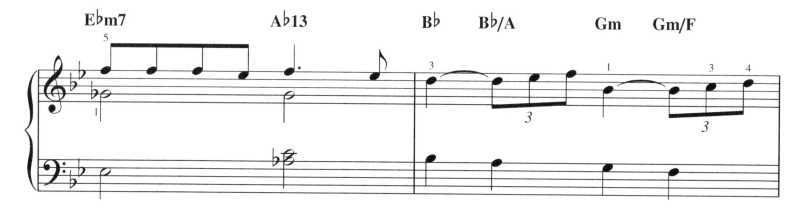

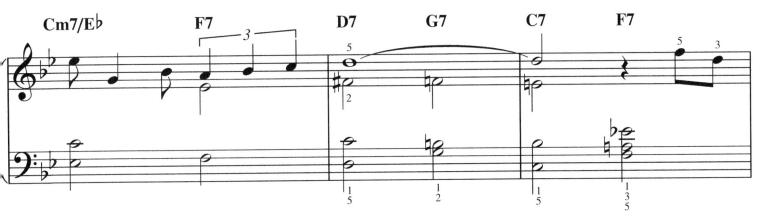

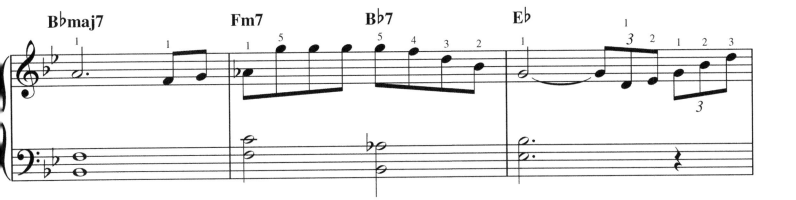

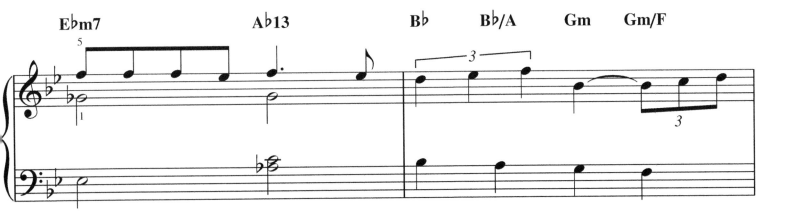

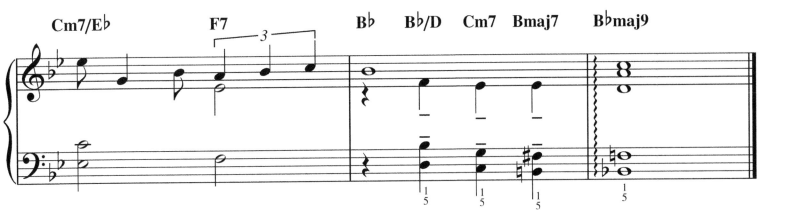

MY WAY

English Words by PAUL ANKA
Original French Words by GILLES THIBAULT
Music by JACQUES REVAUX and CLAUDE FRANCOIS

Resolutely ♩ = 76

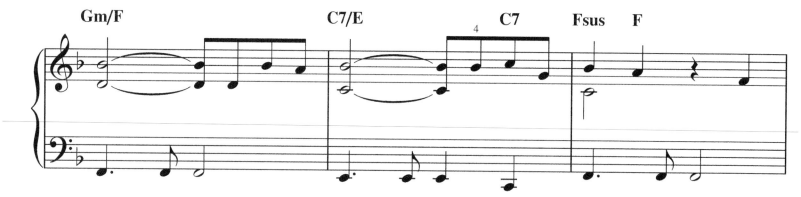

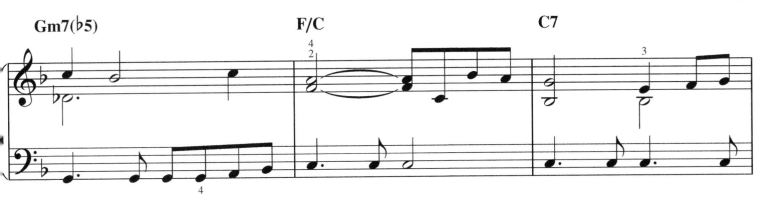

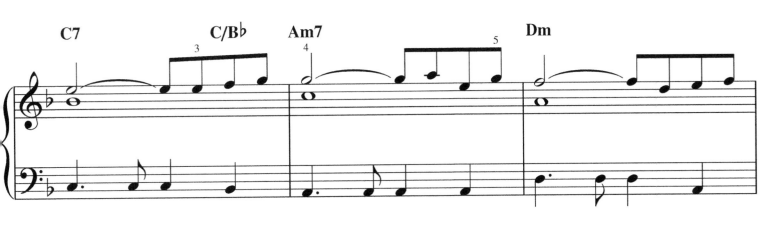
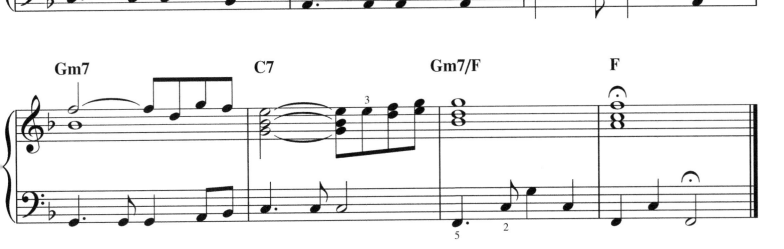

NO MATTER WHAT

from Walt Disney's BEAUTY AND THE BEAST: THE BROADWAY MUSICAL

Music by ALAN MENKEN
Lyrics by TIM RICE

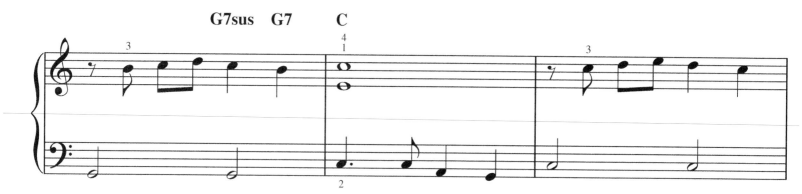

SACRIFICE

Words and Music by ELTON JOHN
and BERNIE TAUPIN

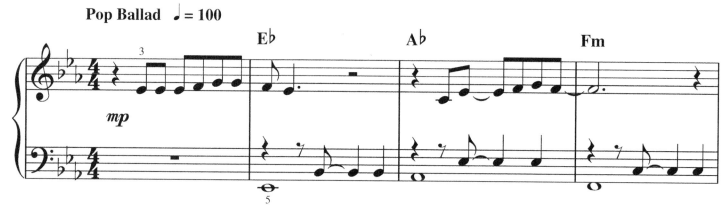

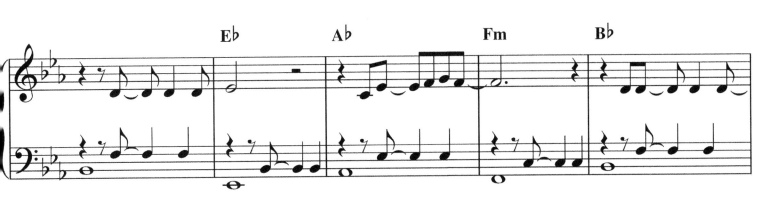

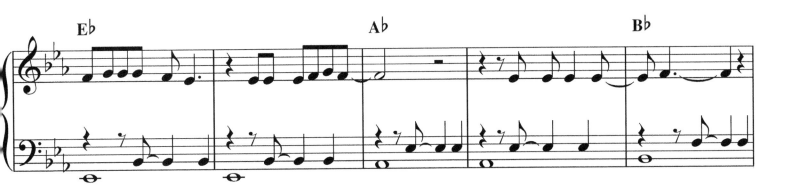

SMOKE GETS IN YOUR EYES

from ROBERTA

Words by OTTO HARBACH
Music by JEROME KERN

Moderately, with expression

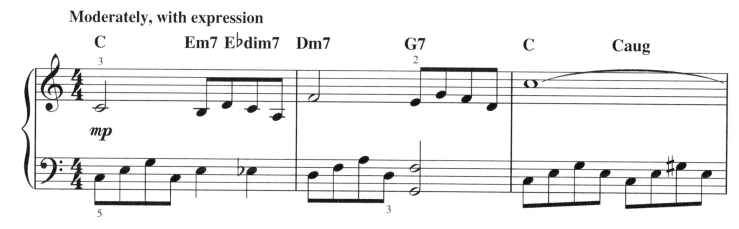

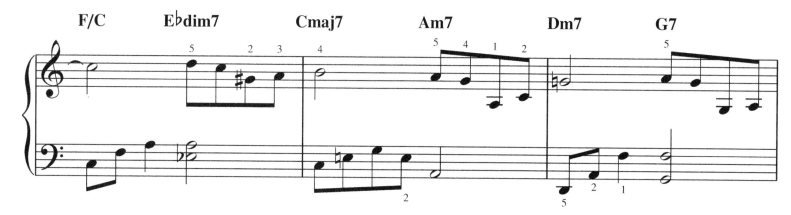

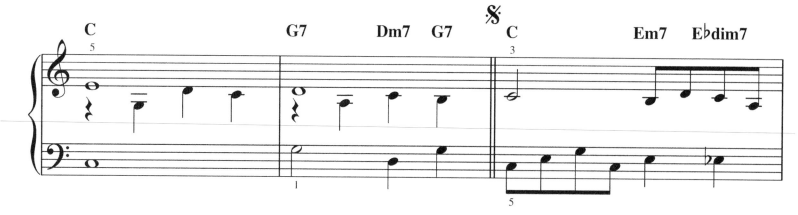

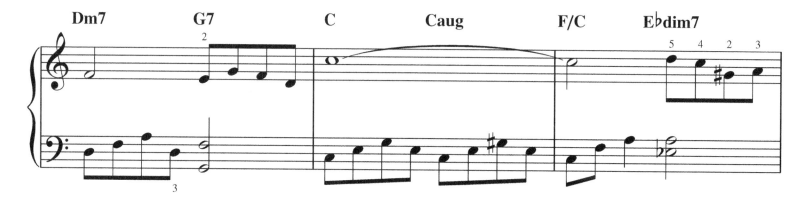

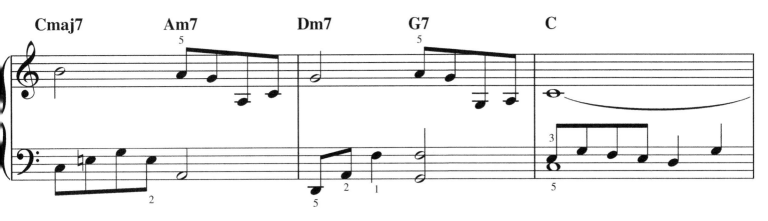

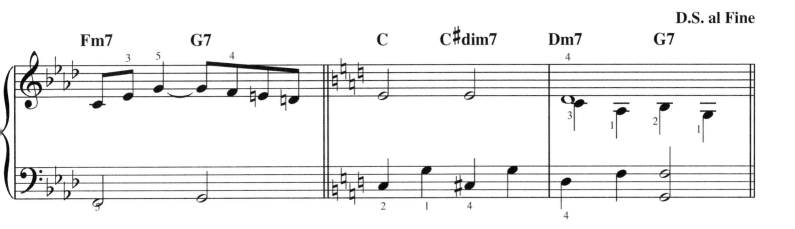

THIS YEAR'S LOVE

Words and Music by
DAVID GRAY

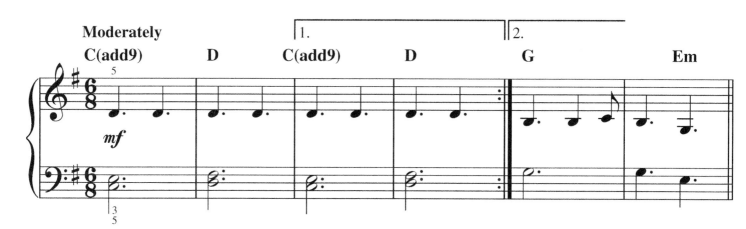

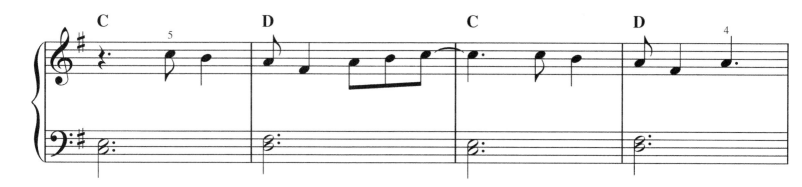

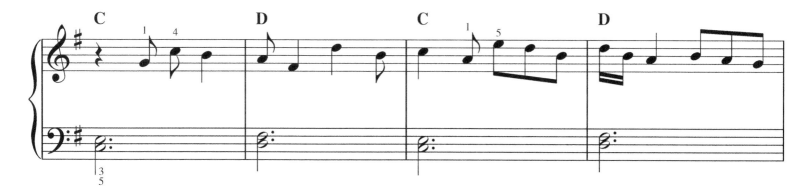

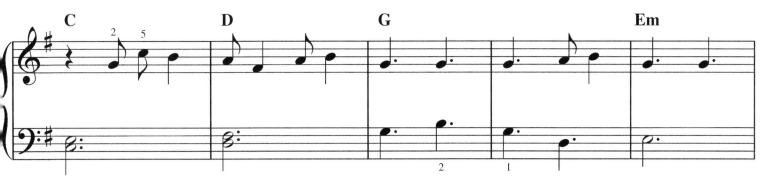

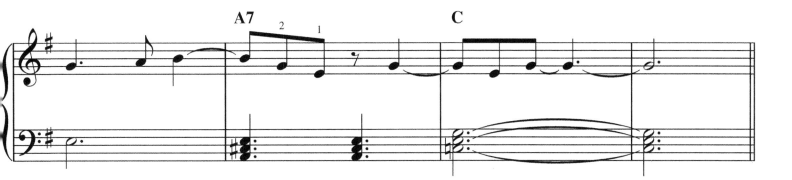

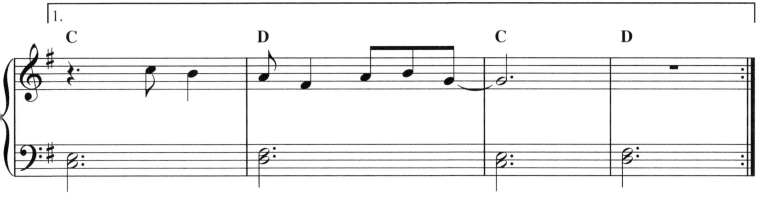

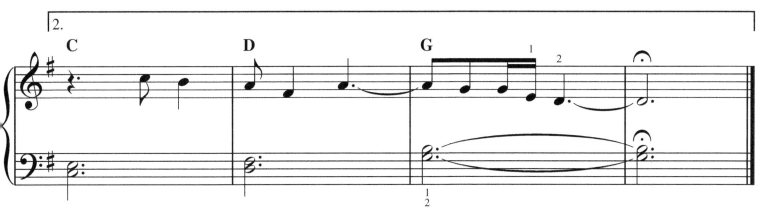

WHAT A WONDERFUL WORLD

Words and Music by GEORGE DAVID WEISS
and BOB THIELE

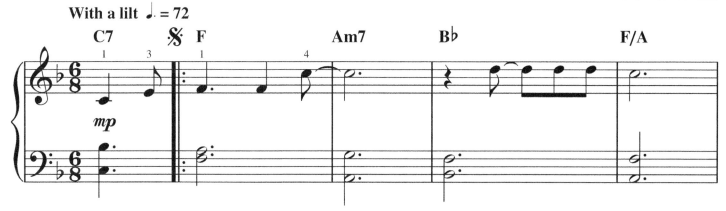

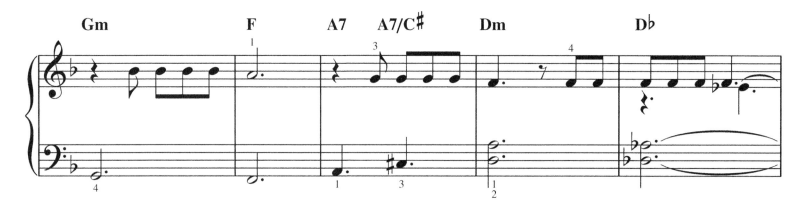

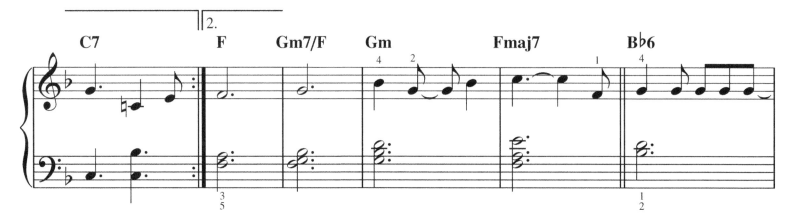

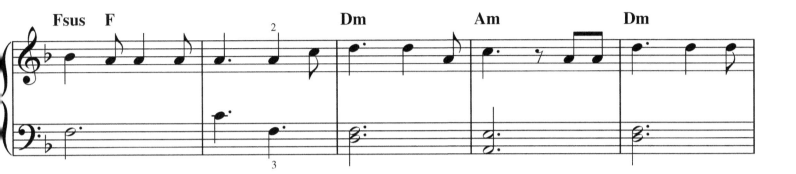

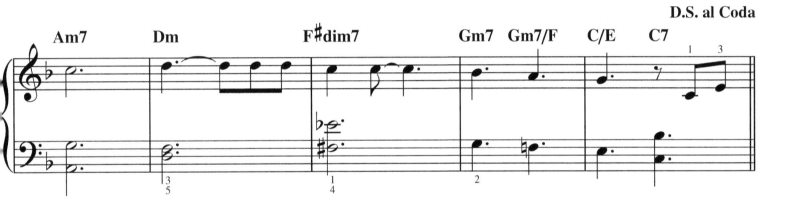

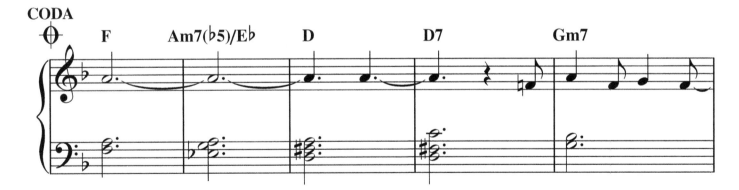

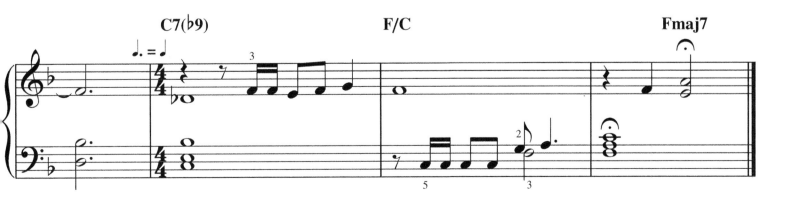

WHEN YOU SAY NOTHING AT ALL

Words and Music by DON SCHLITZ
and PAUL OVERSTREET

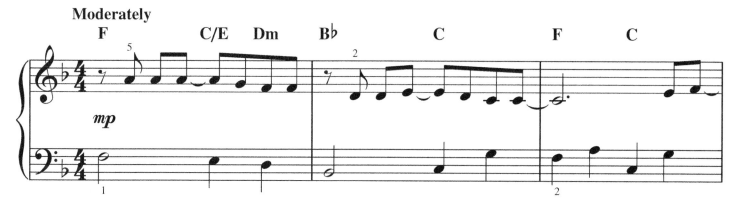

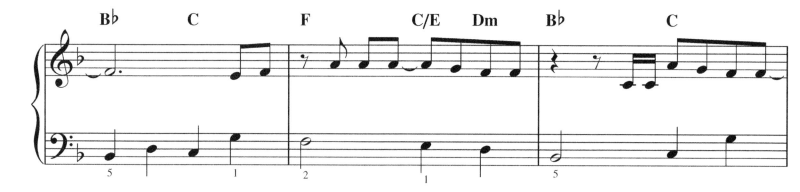

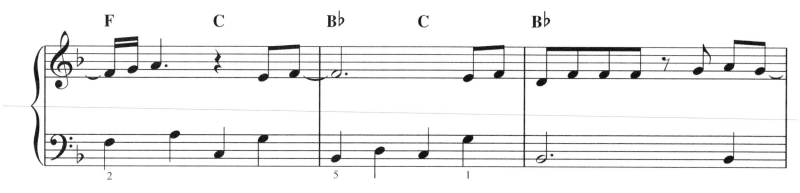

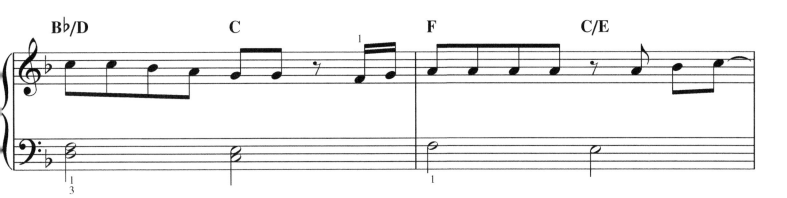

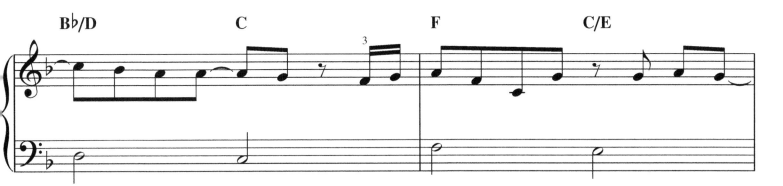

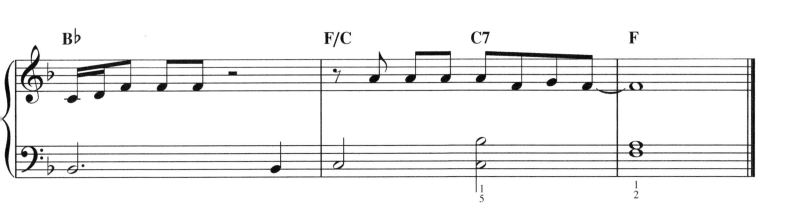

WONDERFUL TONIGHT

Words and Music by
ERIC CLAPTON

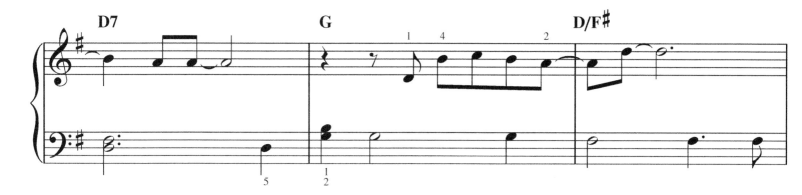

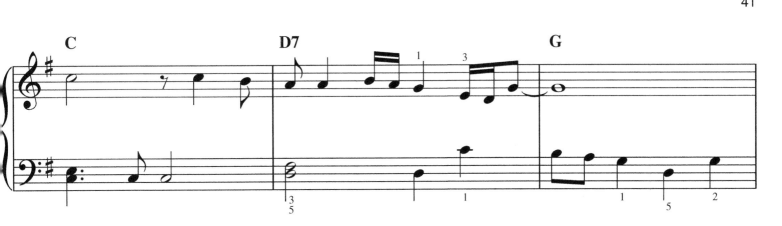

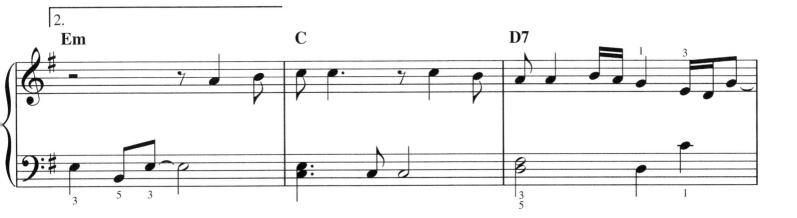

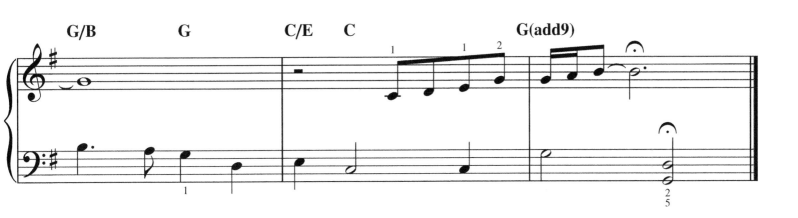

I WILL ALWAYS LOVE YOU

Words and Music by
DOLLY PARTON

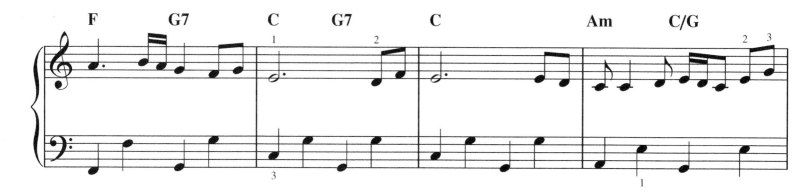

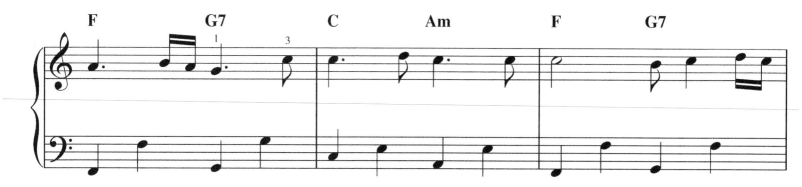